# ideas for Creative Evangelism

## Osi Agboaye

# Ideas for Creative Evangelism

Copyright © 2010 Isi Agboaye
Step Out Creatives Publication,
Birmingham, UK

ISBN: 978-1-906963-03-3

Scriptures taken from the HOLY BIBLE, NEW INTERNATIONAL VERSION®. NIV ®. Copyright ©1973, 1978, 1984 by International Bible Society. Used by permission of Zondervan. All rights reserved.

For copies of this book, workshops and seminars, contact: stepoutmails@aol.com
Phone: 07817629683

Printed in Great Britain

# Dedication

**To the memory of Professor Sonny Oti:**
a great teacher, actor, writer, singer &
friend, who made me see why the show
must always go on in that little
Experimental Theatre.

# Introduction

## What is Creative Evangelism?

Creative evangelism is the use of innovative means to preach the gospel. It could also be described as the method of sharing or communicating the gospel imaginatively. To achieve these goals, artistic ways that appeal more to the five senses should be adopted in order to craft meaningful ideas in the minds of those to whom we are ministering.

In considering creative evangelism, we should comprehend how the mind works and appreciates things that are artistically crafted, with definite outcomes. That is why Hollywood films and the music industry have creatively held the world bound for ages, as they dictate and direct the pace of popular culture by stealing the minds of our youth. So we must perceive the larger picture and choose to be creative.

Let's put all available resources towards the production of programmes and activities that are creative and useful for evangelism. We should also begin to reach the postmodern audience and creatively develop ideas that would minister to their minds.

If we think that we can favourably share the gospel in old wine skins, we must think again. The message of salvation must be coded in well-constructed pockets which are recognisably relevant; artistically viable and meaningful.

The beauty of the gospel is that the message (deep-rooted in scriptures) remains the same but the method of disseminating it can change. The mission is to be authentic yet relevant in reaching our neighbourhoods, schools, streets, prisons, offices and homes; through the use of radio, television, stage and film.

The task of creative evangelism is beyond the pages of this book. We must commit to creatively preach the word of God and make a declaration that heaven will be willing to sustain.

# Being Pro-active and Creative

Some non-Christians unpleasantly used the buses on the streets of London and other major cities in the United Kingdom to denigrate the name of our Holy God. Although their method was creative, we should challenge them by being pro - actively creative.

Thank God for the various creative methods and programmes through which the gospel has been presented for many years; including the use of music, drama and dance. They are useful; but we must seek to make them much more relevant in terms of content, setting and style.

We must look beyond the traditional ways and means of using expressive arts in the church; we must ask the Holy Spirit to write new scripts in our hearts which will enable us to transmit His message to our intended audience.

## Locating our Audience

We should begin to define and differentiate our audience. We should not apply the same message to everyone. We should begin to meet with our audience where they are - children, women, including single parents; men of various definitions and needs; the disabled, deaf, blind; young people of diverse affiliations and cultures, the old, with different needs; including cultists and folks of other religions or even atheists. The question is, how can we creatively reach them all?

## What does the Bible say?

In **1 Corinthians 9:22**, the Apostle Paul states,

> "to the weak became I as weak, that I might gain the weak: I am made all things to all men, that I might by all means save some".

This verse shows that there is need for creativity and authenticity in the church; there is something we can do.

# Ideas for Creative Evangelism

In **Colossians 4:6,** Paul reminds believers that our conversation should always be full of grace, seasoned with salt, so that we may know how to answer everyone. We may infer from this scripture that it is the duty of Christians to use creative ideas as we engage with all sorts of people.

Furthermore, in the gospel of **Matthew 9:37-38,** our Lord Jesus informs us that the harvest is plentiful, but the workers are few. We are told to ask the Lord of the harvest to send out labourers into his harvest field. The AMPLIFIED BIBLE suggests that labourers be forced into the harvest fields.

## Who was the greatest Creative Evangelist?

Our Lord Jesus used storytelling to reach his audience; and knew when to feed them. There is fun and authenticity in storytelling; that is why Chick Publications made such positive impact in the 1970s and 80s with simple captivating cartoons.

We must seize the opportunity to use new technology; create games that would beat secular ones and put them to shame in their own art. We should strive to make Christian creative arts appealing, so that many will pick it as first choice.

## Defining Church Outreaches

We must see church outreaches in a new light:

a. New settings rather than the regular church space.
b. New resources that would appeal to those who cannot stand our traditional stance.

## Defining Evangelistic Resources

Our resources must be unique. The tracts must assume a new look. Should they also be electronic? Certainly. We need the help of the Holy Spirit as we develop and use resources. Evangelism cannot be static and should not rely on old methods and images.

# Ideas for Creative Evangelism

We should look unto God to pour out a new anointing on us, so that we can produce new ideas that will touch hearts and win souls. This book is a functional tool for all Christians who seek to see souls won into God's kingdom.

# How to use this book

This book shows many Acts that can be performed anywhere. So churches, ministries or individuals may decide to use any of the Acts for their creative evangelism project.

It is suggested that most of the acts should be improvised; however, the true essence and artistic quality should be maintained.

## Creative Evangelism Projects

Churches and ministries should have groups actively designated for creative evangelism.

    a.  It will be important for groups to discuss the various Acts and find out how they may be relevant to their church or ministry.

    b.  They should brainstorm on the sort of characters they would need to perform the Acts.

    c.  They should also explore the cost of putting up the Acts and how to manage the anticipated cast and audience.

    d.  The workshops should also consider

the training needs of the anticipated cast and how to recruit them within churches.

e. The laws and by-laws related to street performances must be carefully explored. Knowledge of areas that are open or restricted to the preaching of the gospel in any city where they plan to reach must be acquired.

f. Prospective cast members should also be trained to know what to expect from any audience. They must develop the tact of knowing how to work in cross cultural settings.

The Acts in this book may be modified or adapted to meet the needs of any group performing or reaching any area, town or city. Moreover, it is advised that the essence of prayer projected in the text should be encouraged by all groups.

These Acts are very useful for evangelism; the devil will not fold his arms and watch us make great gains as we reap souls from the jaws of hell. We must back all performances

# Ideas for Creative Evangelism

with prayer sessions to destroy the works of the evil one.

Finally, let's develop a structure that would enable us to explore the various Acts in this book. For example:

- One specific Act may be projected monthly or yearly in the community.
- It is possible to run two or three Acts in a particular church or ministry at the same time.
- The cooperation among churches and ministries highlighted in this text should be encouraged.
- Audience participation and feedback should be encouraged.

Attempts should be made to distinguish between the Acts that are relevant to church settings and those that are meant for the streets. The church should have a strategic committee that explores or brainstorms on the sort of Acts that may be relevant to a specific part of the city or people group.

# Act-1

## A New Revelation

Suddenly, the atmosphere changed. The churches in the city were speaking with one voice; the whole city stood at attention. Who started this? That was the question on many hearts. Rather than wait for an answer, all hands were on deck and thoughts in gear - absorbing every idea poured into willing hearts by the Holy Spirit.

There was no time to wait, no time to argue, and no time for procrastination. People functioned supernaturally; praying and receiving ideas from God. When they prayed, their voices sounded beautiful; sparkling and shedding a flurry of goodness. This was a wonderful experience; the much awaited power of God had dawned on the church.

Nobody could explain the state of readiness that greeted all hearts. We were all ready to share everything in common. It was like the

# Ideas for Creative Evangelism

days of old - the days of the Acts of the Apostles. There was the willingness to do that sweet will of God, the willingness to serve, the willingness to tell someone about the saving grace of Christ; to share testimonies. Everybody was focussed and ready to be used of God.

It suddenly dawned on the whole Church that they had neglected their prayer posts. So prayers rained from lips. The heavens were truly opened as there was a release to pray and seek the face of God.

The more we prayed, the more the grace of God was poured into our hearts. It was happening everywhere; in all Churches - all ministries, everywhere. We all had a single mission; to raise the banner of Christ - to spread the goodnews that Jesus saves, that our saviour is alive, that He is coming back again and willing to set all free from the bondage of sin.

# Act-2

## More Prayer and Praise

The prayer storm continued all over the city; brethren prayed as never before. They implored God for direction as they saw the weight of ideas that God had released over the churches. They prayed their hearts out and would not stop asking for God's mercy and wisdom.

The praying was punctuated by praise and worship sessions where many thanked God for what He was about to do. They acknowledged that they had no power of their own to accomplish the task of reaching the city. They believed that God was about to do great things by pouring out amazing inspiration on Christians, so that the work of evangelism would be facilitated. Did God respond? Without doubt, God showed up and inspired His children with loads of ideas.

# Act-3

## The Prophetic shower

Ten years earlier, one Sister Major, a diligent and seasoned prayer activist, had prophesied that God was about to move in the city. No one took her seriously. However, at the appointed time, the pastors in the city had no choice but to remember God's word through the humble sister. They rose in one accord to reach the city, making great plans and working in unity to serve the Lord.

There was no time to retreat into the flesh. Men and women, boys and girls, all acted as they were given utterance or revelation by the Holy Spirit. There were groups of brethren from different denominations who gathered to fast and pray. God spoke to His children, giving them ideas in details, with exact specifications. There was so much excitement among the brethren.

# Act-4

## God spoke to Hearts

Many pastors emerged from their prayer closets and endorsed the great move; verifying the fact that they had received a similar vision for the city.

They prayerfully presented their ideas to the elders, who also presented the ideas to the brethren, who received the ideas with a resounding "amen." Church bells chimed.

God was speaking to the church and the leaders at the same time. Songs of praise echoed around the city like thick white smoke coming out of the presence of God. This continued all day. Many hearts were tuned to holiness and there was a call from the presence of God for more consecration. God would not use filthy vessels; He was about to do a new thing - to empower Christians to reach the whole city and the nations with the message of salvation.

# Act-5

## The Pastors' Resolution

This was the day the pastors crafted special resolutions, which were sanctioned by all the elders and brethren. It was a far cry from the disunity and rancour that existed within and between the churches. The resolutions were:

- That all churches in the city must continue to be in agreement, under the direction of the Holy Spirit.
- That doctrine should give way to the leading of the Holy Spirit.
- That the momentum or drive now experienced must be encouraged and not allowed to diminish.
- That they must fully endorse the creative Acts in all the churches.
- That Evangelism would be the main task for all brethren.
- That resources should be poured into all evangelistic projects.

The pastors were particularly thrilled that all churches were totally united in the project. The exciting preparation was an electrifying experience. They just wanted something to happen. The very atmosphere of expectation radiated the brilliance of the soon-to-explode images in the minds of the people.

Every Christian in the city was actively involved. Everybody had something to do; none wanted to be left out.

# Act-6

## They put the Choir on Stilts

One pastor knew that the Choir needed to be projected far beyond what they have always been. Like other members, he felt that they should not just praise God and entertain the local church. The suggestion was that the Choir should be put on stilts - and dressed in the same purple and gold costumes they are known.

The Choir on stilts? What a sight! The whole church agreed that it was a great idea. The church building was too small for them; they were rather more relevant outside the church. The whole city warmed up in excitement; they wanted to see every bit of the Choir as they lapped up their songs and wanted more. It was an interesting spectacle as they walked through the length and breadth of the beautiful city singing songs of praise and projecting the message of peace and joy to all mankind.

# Ideas for Creative Evangelism

This was a wonderful moment that the brethren had never experienced before. The people were thrilled.

# Act-7

## Choirs in Hot Air Balloons

Some churches put their Choirs in hot air balloons. It was such a great spectacle. They sang through the city and made melody all day long. Heads looked up in amazement; some cheered, some just smiled, some waved, and many sang along.

It was interesting to watch the Choir on clipped-on-wings. This was a new and amazing dimension. Many were compelled to listen and participate, singing songs and choruses with so much gusto. They had come at such a time when the city wanted something exciting.

There was hardly any scepticism about their appearance in the city; perhaps the prayers and fasting opened the doors to many hearts. Eyes looked upward to the Choir, as they glowed with incandescent radiance.

# Act-8

## Tambourines for Christ

Some performers in the churches used the tambourine in a new way that exceeded previous demonstrations. They raised the profile of evangelism as they sang and danced to the glory of God. It was possible to imagine, once again, how it was in the wilderness for Miriam and other women who praised God for His wonderful miracle, as the people crossed the Red Sea.

There was no need to give out tracts or preach a sermon. The songs and the tambourines said it all. It was energetic, anointed and graceful. The press was around as the groups ministered in the city. There was a consensus of opinion from the newspapers, that the Christians were playing a major role in the city more than before.

# Act-9

## New Songs

News had spread far and wide that the songs from the Christian artistes had taken over the national chart. Men, women and children sang the songs, and even dogs wagged their tails as the songs were played over the airwaves.

The lyrics were captivating and different. There was a supernatural intervention in the content; as the highlighted scriptures kept people thinking all day long.

Heads swayed from side to side anywhere the songs were heard. Live performers belted out jazz, reggae, calypso and soul pieces to the admiration of hundreds of people in the city. They were all grafted with scriptural themes. All the churches in the city had cooperated in the recording of the songs and the artistes were so pleased that many souls were saved through their efforts.

# Act-10

## Taking a stand on open-top Buses

As soon as the whole city saw the Choirs on open-top Buses, people realised that they had been hit with a new dimension of Christian experience. Many folks went to see for themselves and continued to speak about what was going on in the city. Church leaders wondered why they had not started much earlier. Occupants of the buses could not resist joining in - clapping and singing.

The young and old evangelists had easy tasks; they were not bombarded with too many questions - the songs said it all. In some cases, they had to comfort some of the occupants of the buses who were weeping profusely because they were touched by the lyrics of the songs. Some just wanted to touch the garments of the Choir members. Many hugged them with excitement.

# Act-11

## The Jolly Evangelism Boats

Then the Choirs moved into the Jolly boats. They made the marina a more attractive place once again, providing a level of performance that could not be ignored. Their songs were inspiring and the message was compelling. It was so exciting to hear those wonderful voices rise and fall with the waves.

Folks who had fun by the seaside saw the outing of the Choir as an added bonus. Being a neutral setting, the good news of the gospel was received with open hearts. Why? Because the church had dared to move to the people, rather than the reverse.

Some elders remembered encouraging the church to move into the communities. However, the level of anointing presently operating in the people was different and profound.

# Act-12

## The Drama Teams moved in

The drama teams were not going to be left out. They were rehearsing intently, putting finishing touches to various performances. Rehearsals were taking place for days and nights. Someone actually suggested that the drama team was dynamic enough to organise shows everyday, wherever and whenever it chooses.

The church authorities thought that the drama group should be located outside the church most of the time. The elders promptly endorsed all the members as permanent members of staff in the church. The news filtered to other churches where the members promptly did the same. With the level of encouragement, the sky was the limit in terms of their ability to produce excellent performances. As soon as the drama teams moved into the communities, the whole city was electrified. They had many interesting productions:

- A play about Noah's Ark was actually performed in an open top vehicle which moved around the city.
- A play about the different miracles of Christ was performed at the city centre.
- There was a play about the crossing of the Red Sea by the Israelites.
- There was a play about the Second Coming of Christ.
- There was a play about the encounter between David and Goliath.
- There were plays about issues that many folks encountered in the city, relative to drugs, prostitution, crime, homelessness, family values, etc.
- There were plays about other themes in the Bible, and many souls were touched.

# Act-13

## Women Really Aglow

In this atmosphere of excitement and creativity, women were targeted to be reached with various programmes. However, whereas they were seen as a block of people, there was the need to differentiate them so that they could be reached effectively.

- nursing mothers
- single mothers
- working mothers
- women in high flying careers
- those who were disabled
- homeless women
- stay-at-home mothers, etc

Differentiation encouraged the church to know how to plan programmes for the women and create resources to evangelise them effectively. As a result, many souls were reached among the women.

# Act-14

## Great Expectations

Non-Christians were always looking forward to the next show. They gathered at specific show areas even before the performers arrived. There was always something to look forward to. Imagine non-Christians looking forward to seeing a play that is comparable to what they would watch at the London West End, or the New York's Apollo Theatre.

Regular well-written plays and improvised ones were planned and enacted. It was so exciting to know that the drama groups performed at different areas in the city. They explored different themes based on different needs of the people. It was so interesting to see how they flipped from one topic or theme to the other. Tears flowed freely and many fell on their knees, asking forgiveness from God.

# Act-15

## Robots Acting

Scientists in the churches had achieved a feat by creating robots that acted on the streets. This brought a great dimension to Street Theatre with a lot of excitement. At certain times, the robots would also perform with human performers.

What was equally interesting was that the robots spoke, acted and performed unbelievable feats that astounded many folks on the streets.

The scripts were written around the robots and the themes were very relevant. Some institutions welcomed and integrated their art into their programmes. They shone as light in the dark and did not go Bible-bashing. Many who saw their performances wanted to be in church the following Sunday. That was so amazing.

# Act-16

## Puppet Theatre on the Church Roof

On one of the days, a Puppet Theatre performance took place on the roof of a church. Many people in the city had never seen such a phenomenon before.

Many stopped to see what was going on. The amplification was excellent. The themes that the puppets addressed reflected the people's needs.

Some just stood there watching endlessly and enjoying the moves by the puppets. There was singing, dancing and various unusual acts by the puppets.

The themes were specifically relevant as the ideas mirrored issues that touched the hearts of the people. There was audience participation although they could not climb to the roof tops.  It was spectacular.

# Act-17

## Mobile Book / Counselling Caravans

Some specially-constructed caravans served as book and counselling posts for people of all groups. The activities of the mobile caravans are reminiscent of the Operation Mobilisation missionary ships, (Logos and Doulos) that sail around the world selling books and ministering. The caravans moved through the city offering Library and other services including:

- Spiritual Counselling
- Career and learning advisory services
- Marriage counselling
- Youth advisory services
- Drugs addiction advisory services

There was a prayer cell within the caravan where folks could be ministered to. There was a long line of people waiting to use the services.

# Ideas for Creative Evangelism

# Act-18

## The Church Stage

The main church services were not left out. The drama groups thrilled the brethren with encouraging, exciting and edifying plays. The performances also illustrated the sermons of the pastors. The impact was tremendous.

The intensity of devotion and praying increased. The performers also spent time praying fervently and drawing inspiration from the Holy Spirit. There was hardly any performance or activity that was not dedicated to the Lord. This re-emphasised the fact that Christ Jesus is the Lord of the harvest.

Audience participation was encouraged once again and the people were confident to debate and share their opinion about the content of the productions.

# Act-19

## Surprise Actors

There were various experimental performers who went about the whole city acting. The actors would walk around as ordinary folks and suddenly begin to dramatise a scene from a play based on:

- Symbolic themes
- Few actors
- Episodic structures
- Short and effective plays

Many folks who had never encountered Christian theatre loved it. It was even more interesting because it was the Christmas season. As they performed, they sowed seeds in the hearts of many; yokes were broken and many were added to the church. Moreover, folks in the city had something to look forward to. Other performers took on the role of stock characters exploring the Christmas message.

# Act-20

## Banners on Light Aircrafts

Light planes took to the sky and displayed massive banners with scriptural verses. The verses were boldly written in various ways:

- Think Heaven
- Jesus is Love
- God loves you
- Jesus is still alive
- Wise folks must lean on Jesus
- Look unto Jesus

Folks in the city were compelled to look skyward, admiring the wonderful array of colours and messages. It was a compelling sight and the hand of God could be seen at work pointing the eyes of millions to the banners and the messages displayed. The light aircrafts also wrote encouraging inscriptions in the sky, inviting folks to attend church on Sunday as well as other church activities.

# Act-21

## Multi-Media Church Services

The churches developed a system whereby church services were broadcast on Cable TV, Radio and Internet simultaneously. The use of electronic billboards also enhanced the message as they appeared in strategic areas of the city.

There were giant electronic billboards displayed on the rooftop of churches and as well as strategic parks in the city. They were a compelling sight; a living Act that projected the wild, the crooked, the funny, the bestial and savage nature of mankind.

There was no need to stop and see the whole picture; a glance was enough to imprint a message. The cross was portrayed, as relevant and precise. Words were precise and loud; actions held the key to valuable meanings and many wondered why the church had hidden the best for so long.

# Ideas for Creative Evangelism

These electronic images became a viable attraction to many who otherwise would like to spend time in sinful or lustful attractions. People had a positive outlet to appreciate the goodness of God; sublime imagery that has for awhile eluded them. Many accepted Christ as Lord and Saviour.

# Act-22

## Great Enactments

Enactments of Biblical themes were rife and particularly interesting. One church had an open-air service and enacted the story of Noah and his Ark. The audience was drenched by rain but not discouraged. They sat or stood through it all. Several responded to the call of salvation; many rededicated their lives to Christ, and souls were saved.

Such was the great interest that welcomed the performances, like the days of great revivals in Wales, Scotland and Azusa. What was equally exciting was that many new converts joined the groups that were ministering; adding to the number of performers. It was obvious that they did not join the teams as a result of the excitement, but because they wanted to be part of the good cause of saving souls.

# Act-23

## Drop-in Services

A pastor's wife organised a drop-in service where people within the community could come into the church at certain times to discuss their problems. She encouraged the women to help provide for the needs of the less fortunate ones in the community.

Folks dropped in and had useful sessions where they presented their needs and problems. The pastor's wife listened intently and her counsel opened the hearts of many to the gospel.

Those whose relatives had gone to war or were deep in drug use had good and encouraging counsel. The church became very relevant in the city and many had reason to be associated with it. The number of people who attended church services increased and many felt genuinely thrilled to be associated with Christians.

# Act-24

## Campus & Prisons Outreach

A specific team was dedicated to reaching out to college and university campuses. Full theatrical performances explored relevant areas that challenged the academia to repentance. A particular performance of Dr Faustus by Christopher Marlowe was very successful and the academics in their ivory tower saw a reflection of their vanity and repented in large numbers.

Drama teams visited prisons and hospital wards with puppet theatres. They were particularly successful because they drew many non-Christians to repentance. Some prisoners were challenged to be Christians; many with long jail sentences set up drama teams.

The atmosphere in prisons had changed. Prison wardens reported that the Christian prisoners reflected positive image and good behaviour.

It was apparent that the messages projected through the performances produced good results in the hearts of the prisoners. More prisoners were given responsible positions in the prison yards and cases of misdemeanour in the prisons had reduced greatly.

# Act-25

## Outstanding African Nights

A few churches had African nights. The programme attracted so many Africans and was extended for many more days. There were activities about Africa. The music, dance, folktales, colours, facial expressions, call-and-response rhythms electrified the church atmosphere. The people kept asking for more.

The different people groups in Africa were represented, doing one cultural activity or the other to the praise of God's name. There were folks from: Guinea, Ghana, South Africa, Cameroon, Ethiopia, Egypt, Cote d'ivoire, Niger, the Gambia, Nigeria, Mali, Malawi, Kenya, Zimbabwe, Tunisia, Senegal, Morocco, Chad, Togo, Uganda, and several other African countries. Their sensational presentation revealed a lot about Africa. There was so much about diversity projected in:

# Ideas for Creative Evangelism

- Energetic Drumming
- Singing
- Rhythmic movements and dancing
- Bright Colourful fashion
- Exotic Foods
- Languages
- Folklore
- Acrobatics
- Well articulated mimes
- Captivating and inspiring music, etc.

These characteristics did not only enliven the beauty of the evenings, but also enhanced the ways that Africans were perceived and reached with the gospel in the city.

# Act-26

## Incredible European Nights

European cultures and traditions were projected in evenings that would normally see the doors of churches closed or normal services not taking place. Cultures and traditions of various European nations were featured. Various Europeans were available for many shows: the Polish, Hungarians, French, Irish, British, Welsh, Spanish, Scottish, Russians, the Dutch, etc.

Like the African evenings, the European evenings exhibited lots of humour and excitement. This radiated the glory, beauty, grace and the awesomeness of God. There was a new wave of revelation about how people felt - and this created a useful perspective in cross cultural evangelism. Whereas folks related differently to each other before these events, there was a new depth of understanding that revealed more about the people.

# Ideas for Creative Evangelism

Above all, souls were saved and added to the Kingdom of God. For the first time, many appreciated coming to church and various communities felt the importance of the local church in their midst.

# Ideas for Creative Evangelism

# Act-27

## Amazing Latin American Evenings

The Latin American evenings showcased all the excitement of the samba and semi carnivals. The atmosphere was awash with colours and radiance. In addition, the historical perspectives of the regions were re-enacted. People learnt why and how Latin Americans struggled to liberate themselves from all sorts of oppression and domination.

Many folks from the Latino community were excited that the church took interest in them. They rejoiced in the saving power in the blood of Jesus to heal and to save. At the end of the shows, many Christians resolved to visit Brazil, Guatemala, Cuba and other Latin American countries because of the beauty and exquisite expressions that were revealed. The foods were exotic and many confessed that they were tasting such palatable cuisine for the first time.

# Act-28

## Fantastic Oriental Evenings

The Oriental evenings had a lot in store in terms of cultural performances. The Chinese, Koreans, Japanese and many others came with a lot of excitement and flavour.

The cultures were expressive and colourful, showing the goodness and greatness in God's diverse world. Many came from far and near to see the glory of God displayed on a large scale.

Apart from the music, dance, acrobatic displays and humour, issues from the region were explored and analysed from a Christian perspective.

The whole atmosphere was truly moving and blessed. There was so much to eat and drink as brethren and others sampled meals from the region. The pastor used the opportunity to minister to the brethren.

# Act-29

## Awesome American Evenings

The churches organised evenings that explored American history from the earliest times to the present. There was a lot on the Industrial Revolution and the development of labour unions

The music was electrifying as the roots of various forms of music: soul, Jazz, rock, R&B, etc, were traced to particular sub-groups in the American principality. There was so much said about the revivals.

There was a futuristic enactment that portrayed America as a nation that relegated God to the background, despite all that He had done to bless the nation. People prayed and remembered 2 Chronicles 7:13-14:

> *If I shut up heaven that there be no rain, or if I command the locusts to devour the land, or if I send pestilence among my people;*

# Ideas for Creative Evangelism

*If my people, which are called by my name, shall humble themselves, and pray, and seek my face, and turn from their wicked ways; then will I hear from heaven, and will forgive their sin, and will heal their land.*

The outcome of the performance was that America was spared. There was healing, repentance and restoration of its past glory as America gave glory to God and honoured His institutions. At the end of the show, many were saved and many dedicated their lives to God.

# Act-30

## Marvellous South Asian Evenings

Folks from India, Bangladesh, Pakistan, Sri Lanka, had a wonderful evening of Music, dance, recitals; all linked to the scriptures. The exciting thing was how the cultural images were woven around performances through which the gospel was preached. From one of the regions, the traditional drums rolled, the footsteps moved with agility and meanings were conveyed.

The beauty and colours of the region inspired many; especially as the word of God was expressed through those cultural images that drew many to the church.

The gastronomic display was excellent as many tasted and enjoyed Asia's exotic foods. Many who attended had the opportunity to receive Christ as Lord and saviour.

# Act-31

## Grand Caribbean Evenings

The fireworks and excitement that greeted the Caribbean evenings were awesome.

There was a great photographic display of the various Caribbean countries.

- There was so much to learn
- So much to eat
- So much to hear in terms of the music
- The carnivals were awesome; projecting colours and vitality, reminiscent of great carnivals in Brazil and London. It was a memorable experience.

These evenings attracted many folks from far and near. A great number of those who were invited were so thrilled that they joined the local church. As a result of the success, this programme was replicated in other churches in the city and many were saved.

# Ideas for Creative Evangelism

The sound of steel drums echoed in the large auditoria of the churches which had since been expanded to accommodate more members. At a particular period the services could no longer be held in the local churches; but were transferred to the city stadium with excitement and camaraderie.

There were no inhibitions. This openness prompted the folks to ask useful questions. This led to the appreciation of the great cultures from the Caribbean islands. There was great revelation about the needs, feelings, and history of the people. This created a better understanding and the channelization of the gospel of Christ to many hearts.

What was more interesting and memorable was that the people who in the evenings wanted more. There was no evening that was not occupied with one activity or the other. There was loud music, dance, and most in the congregation joined in the performance.

# Act-32

## A Day of Fasting and Prayer

On this day, brethren from all the churches dedicated themselves to prayer and fasting. There was no performance or activity of any sort. Brethren prayed fervently in all the churches and lifted their requests to God. The pastors, elders and brethren successfully coordinated activities related to fasting and praying.

- The attendance was encouraging.
- The people prayed wholeheartedly.
- The brethren prayed about all the activities, imploring God to intervene and open the hearts of their audience.
- They asked God to set captives free and to destroy every bondage of Satan.
- They asked God to protect all the Christian performers, and a release of more inspiration by the Holy Spirit; and the ability to reach more souls for Christ.

# Act-33

## Writing Competitions

This was another good idea to open the hearts of many young people to Christ. The churches organised competitions centred on creative writing in the following areas: Poetry and play writing; song writing, novel and short story writing. Many folks, particularly the young ones, participated with so much excitement.

The topics for the contests centred on practical issues which aroused the interest of many. When the results were released in the church hall, many people, Christians and non Christians attended to enjoy the reading of the brilliant pieces of writing that were created.

The prizes were good. They included shields, silver trophies and medals which were proudly worn by the winners. At the end, many souls were won to the Lord.

# Act-34

## The Talent Hunt

There was a specific show organised in churches to seek out and train talents. Many Christians and non-Christians participated and their talents were identified, put to good use and classed into the following areas:

- Song writing
- Drama
- Dance
- Singing
- Drumming
- Writing
- Poetry
- Rap music
- Fine Art
- Juggling, etc.

Many mature Christians who thought they had nothing to offer demonstrated great talents. The show attracted many onlookers and highlighted the message of salvation and deliverance.

Participants took part in various displays; as a result, a number of talented Christians were identified.

There was a case of a seventy-year-old man who had been in the church for more than fifty years and had hardly contributed anything to the activities. He confessed that he had never been inspired to use his talents. When he started to sing and play the banjo, people clapped and danced. As soon as he stopped, he started playing again. With the excitement in the air, many more were inspired to reveal and use their talents.

This programme became an exciting hub for evangelism and many people were invited to enjoy the activities; as a result many came to the saving knowledge of Christ.

# Act-35

## Spectacular Sky shows

There were spectacular night shows; as had never been seen before in the city. People would gather in front of their houses or just sit on their balconies to experience the expressive shows in the sky.

Bible verses and characters would appear in the sky. There were even some dramatic performances projected on the sky. The scientists in the churches had teamed up to create the spectacular 3D displays with acts that had the following characteristics:

- Colourful features
- Cartoon characters
- Images and ideas that tickled the imagination of onlookers.

Some shows that had taken place earlier in the day were projected in the night sky with thrilling outcomes. Fireworks and visual images were incorporated into the nightly shows.

# Ideas for Creative Evangelism

In all these, the message of the gospel was carefully intertwined with displays that produced excellent outcomes.

People enjoyed the show so much so that they started making requests for specific themes to be added. The organisers focused on either the New or the Old Testament as themes for the night; creating awe-inspiring experiences shown thus:

- We saw Moses and the Israelites crossing the red sea.
- We saw Jonah in the belly of the Whale.
- We saw many miracles of Christ and His image came alive in the sky.
- We saw the creation of the world and all the elements that makes the book of Genesis unique in the Bible.
- We saw the Acts of the Apostles re-enacted.
- We saw Joseph and the whole story about his experience in Egypt.

- We saw Daniel in the den of Lions where God spared his life.
- Biblical quiz and Bible verses were projected.
- We saw David defeating Goliath.
- We saw angels and the vivid imagery of heaven as well as the crucifixion, death and resurrection of Christ.
- We saw aspects and pictures of the Welsh, Azusa and Indonesian revivals projected.

Not only were these images spectacular, they also revealed many interesting aspects of the scriptures that many in church and the city have hardly taken notice of.

At certain points during the projection, the images in the sky became more relevant than the television screens in many homes; an opportunity that revealed the gospel to many.

# Act-36

## Odd Clothes & Shoes day

There was a special day in one of the churches where folks were invited to put on odd clothes and shoes. It was very hilarious. The main idea was that folks were allowed to feel free in whatever clothes they chose to put on; which in itself, made the service quite interesting.

The Pastor drew out specific points from the activity:

a. That certain aspects of our lives are odd.

b. That Christ can actually mend those aspects of our lives.

c. That we must be ready to meet the needs of those who might seem odd in our midst; emphasising that Christ died for them also; thus, taking the message of Christ which is centred on peace to them.

Ideas for Creative Evangelism

d. That we should not condemn those who are different from us; but rather provide them a platform for accepting Christ.

The service was very memorable, exciting, colourful and funny. Many folks came in odd clothes, odd shoes; including all sorts of eccentric or outlandish costumes. Despite the nature of the displays, the message was relevant, and souls were saved.

# Act-37

## Rag Day Outreach

This service encouraged members to dress to church in rags. The reason for this was to project the importance of humility in the body of Christ. The message was also used to preach the gospel and to project the fact that Jesus came for all; both rich and poor. Moreover, the need for us as Christians to take care of the lost was emphasised. There was also the need to put ourselves in the place of the poor to experience how they feel.

There were dramatic enactments in the church to project the needs of the poor and to see what poor folks are going through in other parts of the city and the world. An open invitation was given to poor folks in the community to come to church. There was the dramatic enactment of the washing of feet which Jesus did in the scriptures. Other activities included:

69

# Ideas for Creative Evangelism

- The poor were invited to come to the Altar to testify about all that they were going through.
- Many in the congregation came out to wash one another's feet.
- Many were encouraged to give to the poor and to see the poor as part of the church.
- The poor received counselling and were encouraged to believe in the Lord who would lift their heads as they work towards improving their situations.
- Most of those who attended the service were encouraged to take advantage of the open doors in the city. Many came back to testify that they had actually started putting things in motion.
- Prayers were said and the yoke of poverty broken.

# Act-38

## Displaying items of Sentimental value

Some of the brethren suggested that they organise a service centred on bringing items of sentimental value to church. Some brought their favourite books, dolls, toys, and many others to a special service.

Brethren stepped out of the congregation to testify and tell stories about items they brought, and the lessons they learnt through them. One interesting thing was that the testimonies were relevant to others in the congregation.

The non-Christians who attended had the opportunity to listen to the gospel of Christ and see the need to change. Some of the folks left what they brought in the church. This was significant in the sense that many had been delivered from their past. Tears were shed and laughter echoed in the air.

The pastor preached on healing and related the events of the evening to different aspects of the scriptures.

# Act-39

## Service of Hymns

People around the city were invited to a church service to sing. The congregation was encouraged to pick their favourite Hymns. During the service, some members came out to read portions of stories associated with the Hymns.

The service had such a great impact; many gave their lives to Christ and many more confessed that they had never been so relaxed in a church service.

The songs were projected along with visuals - bringing the message close to many hearts. As the pastor ministered and related to the hymns, there were not many dry eyes in the congregation. The songs kept echoing all through the church as many wanted the service to continue.

# Act-40

## Soup Kitchens on Wheels

A group in one of the churches organised Soup Kitchens on wheels for the poor, homeless and vulnerable ones in the city. The Kitchen staff and eating area were all located on the vehicles. They received so much attention that the city government highly recommended the project.

There were about ten Kitchens on wheels moving from one part of the city to another, reaching as many people as possible.

The main thrust of the project was the idea that Christians must show kindness to the less privileged in society. The feeding programme incorporated the rehabilitation of the homeless and ex-prisoners. There was also the need to encourage the users of the programme to actively search for work.

# Ideas for Creative Evangelism

The project encouraged donation of clothing and toiletries from the brethren to the poor.

There were wonderful testimonies. Many folks who used the services came back to church to testify about how the project encouraged them to receive Christ in their hearts. Few months later, some came back to testify that God had opened doors for jobs and new homes; including finding meaning out of their lives.

The project was very popular and many folks encouraged the organisers of the Kitchens to visit their areas. In some cases, people waited in queues for about an hour before the Soup Kitchens arrived. As soon as they arrived, one could see the glow on faces as they filed through to take their seats in the vehicle. They were treated to two-course meals which they will always remember; a manifestation of the deep kindness of some brethren in the church.

# Act-41

## Booster Learning Sessions

One of the churches came up with the idea of supporting students with booster learning sessions. School leavers who had not particularly done well in one subject or the other were tutored and given a second chance to do better in their weak subjects.

There were many booster sessions in different parts of the city, and many young people used the services to their advantage.

Several young people came to church services to testify about the saving power of Christ and the blessings of the free booster learning sessions. Many parents were particularly grateful to the Christian teachers who had volunteered to help the young people to do well in difficult subjects.

One centre recorded more than a thousand hundred pupils, with many teachers who were available to assist them.

These were intense revision and learning sessions. There were encouraging outcomes and many of the young people had personal encounters with the Lord as a result of the ministration that accompanied the learning sessions. Many were greatly thrilled and encouraged.

# Act-42

## Unforgettable Sunday School Services

More than before, children in the Sunday schools were differentiated with a touch of technology. Previous attempt was to project a common lesson. This time, Sunday school teachers made sure that the needs of individual children were put into consideration. Although this called for the use of more resources, it was very effective.

Parents were able to see the difference between what their children were and what they became. Moreover, there were various activities that the children enjoyed.

Apart from the usual Sunday school Bible lessons, the teachers placed emphasis on skills development. Some of the children enjoyed kinaesthetic activities and many other resources that were made available to them.

# Ideas for Creative Evangelism

Various themes were included in the lessons, and most of the children were thrilled and willing to attend the sessions. The churches knew that they were putting their funds in the right place and their investment paid off.

# Act-43

## Outreach to the Disabled

There were specific services in the churches dedicated to the disabled. People with different needs were invited to the church services to enjoy the presence of God - putting their individual needs into consideration.

The service was tailored to meet the needs of the blind, those with spinal injuries, the deaf and those with learning difficulties, They all came and were excited to participate in the programme.

Packages and resources were relevant to specific needs; there was a technological feel to things. The equipment needed for the programme was appropriate and readily available to all who subscribed to participate.

This would not have been possible if their needs were not appropriately differentiated.

# Ideas for Creative Evangelism

There was Quiz, music, drama, reading, games, etc. The presence of God was felt during the programme and the people were blessed.

# Act-44

## Sports Spectacular

Some churches used the medium of sports to reach out to souls for Christ. They had inter-church tournaments which attracted non-Christians in the city.

This was a programme which attracted many to the kingdom of God. The way in which the events were organised glorified the name of God and many who would normally not attend church services participated in the sports activities which included: football, table Tennis, hockey, Handball, snooker, etc

The Sport events at church were new and interesting. The participants also had the opportunity to appreciate new sports that had Biblical images and characters. The football games attracted many people.

83

# Act-45

## Old Pictures Day

Some brethren came up with the idea of having a service where old pictures would be exhibited in the church. Each person came forward to speak about the significance of the picture they brought.

The brethren spoke with nostalgia; there were so much tears and laughter. The leaders were able to link the pictures to the scriptures. The imagery reflected centred on:

- Family life
- Fun pets
- School trips, etc.

People brought personal pictures that reflected their joys and sadness; including pictures of holidays and of good times in exciting places. Some folks shared pictures about their missionary experiences to unreached tribes. It was a very exciting experience.

# Act-46

## Drive-in Services

Churches in the city collaborated to have services on open grounds. People stayed in the comfort of their cars and participated in the services as they watched images on massive movie screens in front of them. There was enough room for many vehicles - including trucks.

In no time, the people started coming out of their vehicles to sing, clap and dance. One of such events was so thoroughly enjoyed that the programme started at about 8p.m and ended well after midnight.

The pastor could not believe what he saw – a new wave of experience that encouraged him greatly. He reflected on when he almost quit the ministry because the congregation had dwindled to a handful of members.

# Ideas for Creative Evangelism

The evenings were exciting and boosted a time of awareness and relaxation. There were well trained counsellors who attend to the spiritual needs of many who attended the programme.

Many drivers confessed Christ as their personal Saviour and said that they have not been to a church in many years. Some of them said they attended church periodically on festive or special seasons like Christmas, christenings, funerals and weddings.

# Act-47

## Exciting Debates

There were mock religious debates in parts of the city centre. Some pastors stood on soap boxes to expound the scriptures and debate aspects of the word of God systematically. Previously, many Christians would not like to be involved in such a public show. This was reminiscent of the past when John Wesley and his contemporaries spoke boldly in street corners in England.

Many people gathered to listen and were blessed; some asked interesting questions, and once again, the church came to the people in a dramatic way. Many who would normally not be interested in visiting a church had the opportunity to relate with a seasoned preacher who taught and expounded the Scriptures; exploring the historical, political, economic, and spiritual perspectives.

# Act-48

## They put on Dancing Shoes

Some churches had dance sessions, and many folks in the neighbourhood were invited to participate. They danced to various rhythms performed by seasoned Christian bands, belting out the following tunes:

- Jazz
- Highlife
- Reggae
- Calypso, etc

There were boats and ships moored in the harbour with live bands, music and dance. The canals were live with dance bands sessions projecting Christian themes. At intervals there were short testimonies linked to some of the songs being played by the bands. There was hardly any dull moment as many had the opportunity to hear the word of God proclaimed. There were also rave sessions that attracted majority of youths dedicated to Christ.

# Act-49

## Evening of Exotic Foods

Some evenings were dedicated to the tasting of exotic foods from different parts of the world like, South and North America, Asia, Africa, Australia, the Caribbean, Mexico, Europe, the Middle East, etc.

Many Christians invited their non-Christian friends in the city to attend church services in order to expose them to the gospel of Christ.

The gastronomic experience attracted folks from different parts of the city, particularly international students from universities and colleges around. There were testimonies from many parts of the world and folks related their dishes to their Christian experiences. The project was so successful that the churches decided to stage it once every three months.

# Act-50

## Fancy Clothes Services

Just like the rag day services, some churches organised fancy dress services. The brethren invited their friends and acquaintances to the fancy dress services. The pastors highlighted the importance of glowing in God's glory and the need to radiate the goodness of God.

Most of the brethren dressed to reflect biblical characters. They came out to explain the importance of the characters in which they were dressed. The messages and ideas that came out of the experience were exceptional.

Some of the brethren came out to read relevant portions of the scriptures. The Bible came alive and non-Christians were able to ask questions about the biblical characters that were reflected in fancy clothes.

# Act-51

## Remarkable Tracts & Books

There were teams dedicated to developing tracts that would be relevant to all in the city. The tracts and books were clearly differentiated and relevant to specific audiences. The tracts reflected the following stages of soul winning:

- Sowing
- Watering
- Reaping

There were tracts for different needs and people. The designers of the tracts realised that there are many ways to reach people who have different needs, temperaments and backgrounds. They also saw the need to present the message of the cross in varied and relevant proportions.

The tract team came to realise that a tract with a word or very few words will stick more than one with many words.

## Ideas for Creative Evangelism

Vivid images and cartoons with few words were included in the tracts. Moreover, the tracts had different formats; some were:

- musical
- interactive
- electronic
- funny with exciting cartoon characters
- some were designed as games, etc.

# Act-52

## Extraordinary Youth Outreaches

The youth outreaches were beyond description. There were youth pastors and workers serving a teeming crowd of young people that wanted more.

There were exciting themes hinged on the use of electronic images. Large screens and massive musical equipments gave boost to the exciting outings. There were enough refreshments or places where they could be purchased. The young people sang, danced, dramatised, listened to testimonies, and reflected on issues about development and changes in their life circumstances.

There was hardly a sad face and the atmosphere was very welcoming. Young people with medical issues were adequately helped. There were counselling points and many had the opportunity to ask questions related to career choice.

Courtship, friendship and marriage were regular features. There were sessions on loneliness, the gap year, travels, drugs, sex, crime, etc. These areas were linked to biblical themes and those counselled were relieved. Many enjoyed fellowship with one another as this opened doors to many hearts.

# Act-53

## Medical Outreach

Medical doctors in the churches formed a band of helpers to minister to the sick at their spare time. They volunteered to assist many who had basic medical needs; a practice which relieved the hospitals a great deal, and opened hearts to the gospel.

They did not just operate in the physical; they were endowed with supernatural strength to discern people's ailments. Some had prophetic gifts and many folks marvelled at what the Lord revealed through them.

This opened the doors to the hearts of many who wanted to ask questions about their faith and practice. Many with nicotine, drug, and alcohol addiction had support and were later referred for specialist help which they greatly appreciated.

Daily, people were invited to specific points in the city where they were ministered to.

# Act-54

## The Homeless Team

There were dedicated teams that went about the city meeting the needs of the homeless. They worked closely with the Social Services Department to rehabilitate the homeless. There were cases where some of the homeless people relocated to their previous homes after being ministered to.

There were situations where counselling was offered to the homeless who were on drugs, and others who had problems with various forms of addiction.

The street workers prayed with many homeless folks and befriended them. Some street evangelists had services with them and also invited them to attend their main church activities. Many of them were rehabilitated, and the City Council was very impressed and thanked the street workers for their efforts.

# Act-55

## Jesus Buskers

This team of buskers took the city by storm. They sang great songs and ministered to many. The themes of their songs centred on:

- Salvation
- Deliverance
- Joy in the Holy Ghost
- The vanity of life
- The big void in hearts
- The mercy of God
- The beauty of living in Christ
- Turning it all to Jesus

The buskers danced and sang with a difference and did all they could with smiling faces in order to put their message across. They even told stories of life experiences in ballads. They were such a joy to watch and listen to. Many folks gathered to listen to them as they attracted both young and old. The power in their ministration was very captivating.

# Act-56

## Individual Efforts in the Community

Most Christians opened the doors to their homes and invited friends and neighbours. They had various activities to assist many around them to have encounter with Christ such as:

- Breakfast meetings dedicated to evangelism
- Dinners for evangelism
- Friends and neighbours invited to see home movies
- Wedding ceremonies dedicated to evangelism
- Christening ceremonies dedicated to evangelism
- Barbecues organised for evangelism

The sessions were so effective that brethren came to the church to testify about what God was doing in their home meetings.

# Act-57

## The Jericho March

A quarterly march was organised around the city; many brethren participated. It looked more like a great carnival with lovely floats that depicted various aspects of the Scriptures. Most of the folks on the floats were dressed as Bible characters.

They sang and danced and gave glory to God. Many folks were attracted to the floats which moved and stopped intermittently. There were also many activities for all and there was great opportunity for evangelism.

The floats moved from one part of the city to another and were very dramatic. At the end, the Christians gave a loud shout, similar to the experience at the walls of Jericho.

In our mind's eyes, we could actually see walls of problems crumbling down and God resolving many issues in the lives of people.

# Act-58

## A City-Wide Cleaning Project

The Christians showed up in large numbers to help the City Council clean the city. Through this great example, they were able to minister to several people, and also provided the following:

- Refuse disposal bins
- Refuse incineration plants
- Sign posts that directed city folks to waste disposal points

The Mayor of the city was particularly impressed that he made a special broadcast to thank all the Christians in the city who had contributed to making the city clean. He specifically said that the city was more beautiful because the Christians had come out to partner with the City Council to regenerate various areas. The Mayor also praised the humility of the Christians whom he described as shining lights.

He described them as those who led by example and who practised what they preached. Finally, he thanked them for all they had contributed to make the city a great place.

The Christians also erected visible water fountains which were strategically placed in many parks in the city. New flowers and flower troughs sprang up in different settings. The beauty reflected dazzled and filled the eyes and the sweet smell that oozed from the flowers and plants filled the atmosphere.

# Act-59

## A Middle Eastern Outreach

One of the churches had a special outreach where the brethren from the Middle East were invited to showcase activities from that part of the world. This was an opportunity for many folks to see the common cultural elements from the descendants of Abraham.

There were wonderful faces, lovely music, dance, Mediterranean foods and games. The main highlight was when all the children from the different areas of the Middle East held hands and danced in a circle.

Different dramatic performances were shown to project the blessings and riches of the region and many visitors were touched, as they all prayed for the peace of the region. The evening was very exciting and many people were blessed and it gave the pastor the opportunity to invite many to receiver Christ into their hearts,

# Ideas for Creative Evangelism

Many were excited when a Camel was brought onto the stage. The children were thrilled and many clapped and sang joyfully as the blessings of the region were projected in various art forms.

Ron photo

# Act-60

## Techno-Cyber Invasion

The use of the internet received a major boost in evangelism as many Christians were encouraged to see the power of cyber-culture. Many messages were generated in Social Networking sites as never seen before in their millions. A group of young people in a church had generated thousands of tweets and Facebook messages for Jesus.

Many Christians generated inspiring life saving messages that touched the hearts of many. As a result of the intense messages and interactive activities by Christians, many non-Christians met with Christ and turned their attention from negative areas on the internet, including pornography, gambling and many vices.

Young people spearheaded the cyber invasion and the power of God shone through their activities as never before. Their activities focussed on live prayer sessions, virtual counselling, live chats, and other creative approach of using the internet.

There were games and virtual 3D movies that spoke to many hearts. As a result, many were saved, healed and delivered.

In most of the churches in the city, many Christians became interested in the use of the internet. Many young folks developed new 3D programmes that were compatible with various computers; it was a stunning experience as the Christian community were leading the whole nation in such an innovating computing experience. The most exciting outcome was that many were saved.

# Ideas for Creative Evangelism

# Topics for Creative Evangelism
## Workshops/Seminars

# Appendix 1

**Having read this book, make a list of other creative evangelism ideas that have occurred to you.**

Point:


Point:


Point:


Point:

# Appendix 2
## How important will creative evangelism be to your church or ministry?

Point:

Point:

Point:

Point

# Appendix 3

**Which Acts in this book would you recommend to your church and why? State the reason(s) for your choice.**

Point:

Point:

Point:

Point

# Appendix 4

**What problems do you think Christians may encounter when they use these Acts for evangelism?**

Point:

Point:

Point:

Point

# Appendix 5

## What is the difference between this type of evangelism and others you are used to?

Point:

Point:

Point:

Point

# Appendix 6

**What sort of spiritual and physical preparation do you need to be able to embark on a creative evangelism project?**

Point:

Point:

Point:

Point

# Appendix 7

**Explore the various county or local government licences or permissions you need in your area, in order to organise some of the Acts in this book.**

Point:

Point:

Point:

Point

# Appendix 8

**What are the anticipated financial implications of organising some of the Acts in this book?**

Point:

Point:

Point:

Point

# Appendix 9
**Attempt a breakdown of the cost for some of the Acts.**

Point:

Point:

Point:

Point

# Appendix 10

**How practicable are some of the Acts in this book?**

Point:

Point:

Point:

Point

# Appendix 11
## What is the importance of supernatural manifestation in this type of evangelism?

Point:

Point:

Point:

Point

# Appendix 12

## How would you adapt the Acts in this book to your country or cultural setting?

Point:

Point:

Point:

Point

# Glossary

**African worldview** – the way that Africans perceive issues.

**Audience** – Onlookers or those who watch a play or performance.

**Azusa (Azusa Street Revival)** – Associated with a Pentecostal revival that started in Los Angeles, California in 1906 It was led by William J. Seymour, an African American preacher.

**Calypso** – a Latin American style of Music.

**Chick Publications:** A tract publication company.

**Differentiation:** This is the process of meeting the individual needs of people by providing appropriate resources or using styles appropriate to their needs.

**Dr Faustus** – A play written by Christopher Marlowe.

**Logos and Doulus** – Book selling missionary Ships that sail to different parts of the world spreading the gospel.

**Prophetic:** To be able to predict or tell the future.

**Resources:** Materials that we need for preaching the gospel, like tracts, songs, and other forms of equipment.

**Spectacle:** An unusual display or display of great manifestation.

# Index

# Ideas for Creative Evangelism